THE OFFICIAL
MANCHESTER UNITED
ANNUAL 2013

Written by Steve Bartram and Gemma Thompson

Designed by Jane Massey

A Grange Publication

© 2012. Published by Grange Communications Ltd., Edinburgh under licence from Manchester United Football Club. Printed in the EU.

Photography © www.manutdpics.com and www.actionimages.com

ISBN: 978-1-908925-10-7

£7.99

CONTENTS

Hello and welcome to the 2013 Manchester United Annual

There's no doubt the 2011/12 campaign ended on a disappointing note for everyone connected to the club. Losing the title to Manchester City in the manner we did was very cruel, but we've experienced many ups and downs in the many years that I've been here and most of them have been great moments. Before last season we'd won the league four times in five years and we very nearly did it again last May, but sadly it wasn't meant to be. We take great credit from the fact that despite having so many injuries we were challenging until the very end. We might not always win the league but we're always up there which is great credit to the players, our coaching staff, our sports science staff and our medical team - they've all put a lot into our club.

It's a fantastic achievement to win the Premier League - it's the hardest league in the world and anyone that wins it deserves it. Losing it on goal difference was particularly frustrating and we only have ourselves to blame. We missed too many chances. Obviously we were very disappointed to lose an eight-point lead and there is no doubt that the pivotal match that undid us was the 4-4 draw against Everton, but I'm not going to have any recriminations for any of my players. The young lads will learn from the experiences of last season – both in the league and in Europe - and sometimes a bad experience is better for you. You shouldn't fear the future and these lads won't.

They're a real solid bunch, they're honest and they tried their best. Okay, they've made mistakes but there are a lot of young players who make mistakes and we invest in that. That's what we're good at. We're not like other clubs who spend fortunes. We invest in players who'll be with the club for a long time, who'll create the character of the club and excitement for our fans, and we have many players like that. We're good at that and we're going to continue that way because we want to make sure the evolution of United continues. I've been at the club for over 25 years now and I have to maintain a certain standard that keeps us up there competing for honours every year. We know we'll face another strong challenge in 2012/13 at home and abroad but we're good at challenges and, you can rest assured, we'll kick on.

But before looking forward, it's time to look back one last time on the 2011/12 campaign, as well as reading all about the players – including our new arrivals – and partaking in quizzes that should really test your knowledge of United!

Sir Alex Ferguson

2011

August

Nani begins the players' recollections of the 2012/13 campaign, which started with a dramatic victory over our local rivals at Wembley…

SUN 7 COMMUNITY SHIELD
United 3 Manchester City 2
(Smalling, Nani 2)

SUN 14 PREMIER LEAGUE
West Brom 1 United 2
(Rooney, Reid og)

MON 22 PREMIER LEAGUE
United 3 Tottenham 0
(Welbeck, Anderson, Rooney)

SUN 28 PREMIER LEAGUE
United 8 Arsenal 2
*(Welbeck, Young 2,
Rooney 3 (1 pen), Nani, Park)*

66 It didn't matter to us that we were playing against Manchester City in a friendly when we met them in the Community Shield; a derby match is always a big game and one you want to win. To be losing two-nil at half-time but still come back and get the result so late on is what United is all about – we always play until the last minute. The attitude from the young lads in the second half was fantastic and we all believed that we could do it. It was good to see our new players all play a part in helping us win the trophy; I think David [De Gea], Ashley [Young] and Phil [Jones] were very important signings for us. They settled in very quickly and really added to the team spirit – that's the big thing we have at this club, everybody gets on and fights to be successful together. From a personal point of view the 2010/11 season was definitely my most consistent season and I wanted to build on that so I was delighted to help us win the Community Shield with two goals and to also chip in with another in the 8-2 victory over Arsenal. That game was a great one to be involved in and it rounded off the month in a fantastic manner for us after three important wins in the league. 99

AUGUST STATS
P4 W4 D0 L0
Scored   16
Conceded   5
Clean sheets   1

2011 September

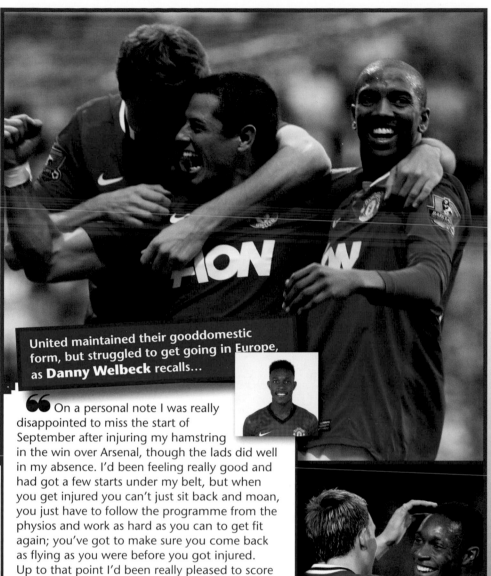

United maintained their gooddomestic form, but struggled to get going in Europe, as **Danny Welbeck** recalls...

66 On a personal note I was really disappointed to miss the start of September after injuring my hamstring in the win over Arsenal, though the lads did well in my absence. I'd been feeling really good and had got a few starts under my belt, but when you get injured you can't just sit back and moan, you just have to follow the programme from the physios and work as hard as you can to get fit again; you've got to make sure you come back as flying as you were before you got injured. Up to that point I'd been really pleased to score a couple of goals and I was delighted to make my comeback in our Carling Cup win at Leeds. Things were going well for us in the league and I was over the moon to score twice in a minute in the Champions League against Basel but we really should have finished the game off after that. Unfortunately we didn't which is just not like us. We didn't start the second half as bright as we should have and that allowed them back into the game and in the end we had to rely on Ashley Young's late goal to get us a point. After drawing our opening game away at Benfica, we knew we'd have to improve and make sure we won our next match against Otelul Galati. 99

SAT 10 PREMIER LEAGUE
Bolton 0 United 5
(Hernandez 2, Rooney 3)

WED 14 CHAMPIONS LEAGUE
Benfica 1 United 1
(Giggs)

SUN 18 PREMIER LEAGUE
United 3 Chelsea 1
(Smalling, Nani, Rooney)

TUES 20 CARLING CUP 3RD ROUND
Leeds 0 United 3
(Owen 2, Giggs)

SAT 24 PREMIER LEAGUE
Stoke 1 United 1
(Nani)

TUES 27 CHAMPIONS LEAGUE
United 3 Basel 3
(Welbeck 2, Young)

SEPTEMBER STATS
P6 W3 D3 L0
Scored   16
Conceded   6
Clean sheets   2

MANCHESTER UNITED

2011

October

SAT 1 PREMIER LEAGUE
United 2 Norwich 0
(Anderson, Welbeck)

SAT 1 PREMIER LEAGUE
United 2 Norwich 0
(Anderson, Welbeck)

SAT 15 PREMIER LEAGUE
Liverpool 1 United 1
(Hernandez)

TUES 18 CHAMPIONS LEAGUE
Otelul Galati 0 United 2
(Rooney 2 (both pens))

SUN 23 PREMIER LEAGUE
United 1 Manchester City 6
(Fletcher)

TUES 25 CARLING CUP 4TH ROUND
Aldershot 0 United 3
(Berbatov, Owen, Valencia)

SAT 29 PREMIER LEAGUE
Everton 0 United 1
(Hernandez)

An important Champions League away win and further progress in the Carling Cup was scant consolation for **Michael Carrick** and co. after a derby day disaster…

" We were all shocked after the City game. Everyone was very quiet and we knew we had to move on straight away. It's always important to look forward to the future, particularly when you have a hard time, and I also think you become stronger for those experiences. We had been doing very well in the league up to that point, but sometimes you have shock results like that and it spurs you on to do better. Every player knew they had to improve and we were pleased to get an important win at Everton in our next league game. Earlier in the month we'd picked up a vital victory in the Champions League away to Otelul Galati. We'd not got the results we wanted in our first two group games so we knew we had to beat Galati who did well on the night. Up to that point I hadn't been involved as much as I'd have liked but after so many years here I know how to deal with that; you just always have to make sure you're ready when the manager needs you. He knows how to encourage all the players, even those you are not playing, and how to use the squad for the good of the team. That's one of his greatest qualities and one which will hopefully continue to make us successful. "

OCTOBER STATS
P6 W4 D1 L1
Scored   10
Conceded   7
Clean sheets   4

SIR ALEX FERGUSON STAND

THE THEATRE

Ryan Giggs reflects on the penultimate month of 2011 as well as paying tribute to Sir Alex as he marked his 25th anniversary as United manager...

66 It's difficult to know how to sum up the manager's achievements at United. Aside from the trophies he's won, he leads by example in everything he does and his work ethic is incredible. He's always first in at the training ground and last to leave, and he wants to see that kind of mentality from his players as well. He just loves his job, loves watching United play and he loves seeing players develop. He's definitely had the biggest influence on my career – he's seen me develop from a 13-year-old to where I am now and he's always been there to support me. It was a great tribute by the club to rename the North Stand the 'Sir Alex Ferguson Stand' before the win over Sunderland. What was even more impressive was the fact the manager knew nothing about it until the unveiling just before kick-off! We followed our victory over Sunderland with another win at Swansea but in truth we didn't play as well as we can. We scored an early goal and then sat back. We suffered another frustrating result in Europe against Benfica and dropping two points at home to Newcastle in the league was disappointing, particularly when the penalty which earned them a point should never have been given. Nevertheless, you always like to think these things even themselves out over the course of the season. **99**

2011 November

WED 2 CHAMPIONS LEAGUE

United 2 Otelul Galati 0
(Valencia, Sarghi og)

SAT 5 PREMIER LEAGUE

United 1 Sunderland 0
(Brown og)

SAT 19 PREMIER LEAGUE

Swansea 0 United 1
(Hernandez)

TUES 22 CHAMPIONS LEAGUE

United 2 Benfica 2
(Berbatov, Fletcher)

SAT 26 PREMIER LEAGUE

United 1 Newcastle 1
(Hernandez)

WED 30 CARLING CUP 5TH ROUND

United 1 Crystal Palace 2
(Macheda pen)

NOVEMBER STATS

P6 W3 D2 L1
Scored   8
Conceded   5
Clean sheets   3

2011

December

SAT 3 PREMIER LEAGUE
Aston Villa 0 United 1
(Jones)

WED 7 CHAMPIONS LEAGUE
Basel 2 United 1
(Jones)

SAT 10 PREMIER LEAGUE
United 4 Wolves 1
(Nani 2, Rooney 2)

SUN 18 PREMIER LEAGUE
QPR 0 United 2
(Rooney, Carrick)

WED 21 PREMIER LEAGUE
Fulham 0 United 5
(Welbeck, Nani, Giggs, Rooney, Berbatov)

MON 26 PREMIER LEAGUE
United 5 Wigan 0
(Park, Berbatov 3 (1 pen), Valencia)

SAT 31 PREMIER LEAGUE
United 2 Blackburn 3
(Berbatov 2)

December started on a high note for **Phil Jones**, but ended on a low for him and his team-mates against his former club on the final day of 2011...

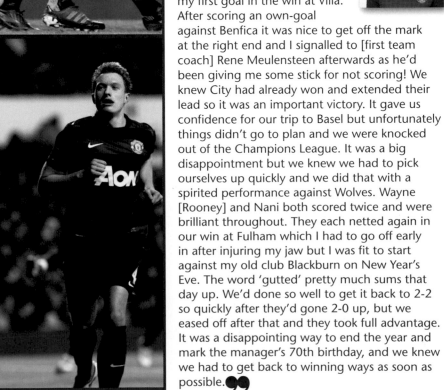

66 I was delighted to score my first goal in the win at Villa. After scoring an own-goal against Benfica it was nice to get off the mark at the right end and I signalled to [first team coach] Rene Meulensteen afterwards as he'd been giving me some stick for not scoring! We knew City had already won and extended their lead so it was an important victory. It gave us confidence for our trip to Basel but unfortunately things didn't go to plan and we were knocked out of the Champions League. It was a big disappointment but we knew we had to pick ourselves up quickly and we did that with a spirited performance against Wolves. Wayne [Rooney] and Nani both scored twice and were brilliant throughout. They each netted again in our win at Fulham which I had to go off early in after injuring my jaw but I was fit to start against my old club Blackburn on New Year's Eve. The word 'gutted' pretty much sums that day up. We'd done so well to get it back to 2-2 so quickly after they'd gone 2-0 up, but we eased off after that and they took full advantage. It was a disappointing way to end the year and mark the manager's 70th birthday, and we knew we had to get back to winning ways as soon as possible. 99

DECEMBER STATS
P7 W5 D0 L2
Scored   20
Conceded   6
Clean sheets 4

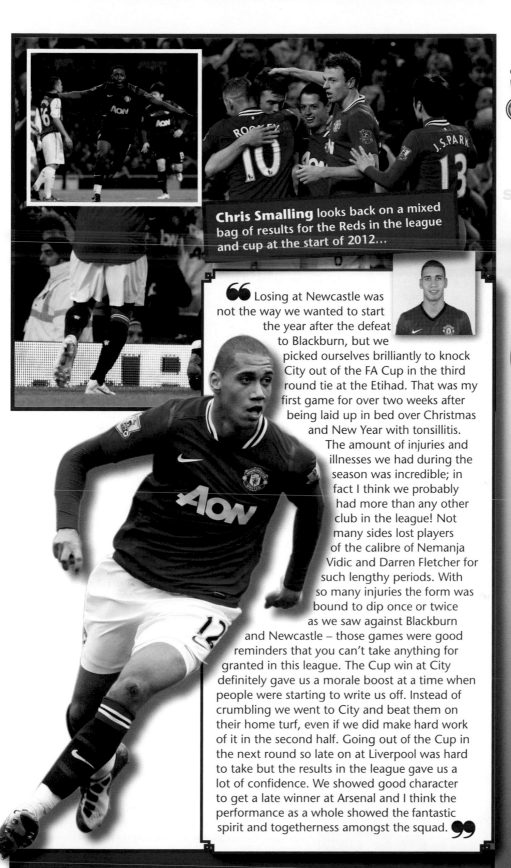

Chris Smalling looks back on a mixed bag of results for the Reds in the league and cup at the start of 2012...

66 Losing at Newcastle was not the way we wanted to start the year after the defeat to Blackburn, but we picked ourselves brilliantly to knock City out of the FA Cup in the third round tie at the Etihad. That was my first game for over two weeks after being laid up in bed over Christmas and New Year with tonsillitis. The amount of injuries and illnesses we had during the season was incredible; in fact I think we probably had more than any other club in the league! Not many sides lost players of the calibre of Nemanja Vidic and Darren Fletcher for such lengthy periods. With so many injuries the form was bound to dip once or twice as we saw against Blackburn and Newcastle – those games were good reminders that you can't take anything for granted in this league. The Cup win at City definitely gave us a morale boost at a time when people were starting to write us off. Instead of crumbling we went to City and beat them on their home turf, even if we did make hard work of it in the second half. Going out of the Cup in the next round so late on at Liverpool was hard to take but the results in the league gave us a lot of confidence. We showed good character to get a late winner at Arsenal and I think the performance as a whole showed the fantastic spirit and togetherness amongst the squad. 99

WED 4 PREMIER LEAGUE
Newcastle 3 United 0

SUN 8 FA CUP 3RD ROUND
Manchester City 2 United 3
(Rooney 2, Welbeck)

SAT 14 PREMIER LEAGUE
United 3 Bolton 0
(Scholes, Welbeck, Carrick)

SUN 22 PREMIER LEAGUE
Arsenal 1 United 2
(Valencia, Welbeck)

SUN 28 FA CUP 4TH ROUND
Liverpool 2 United 1
(Park)

JANUARY STATS
P6 W4 D0 L2
Scored   11
Conceded   8
Clean sheets   2

MANCHESTER UNITED

2012

February

SUN 5 PREMIER LEAGUE
Chelsea 3 United 3
(Rooney (2 pens), Hernandez)

SAT 11 PREMIER LEAGUE
United 2 Liverpool 1
(Rooney 2)

THURS 16 EUROPA LEAGUE LAST 32, FIRST LEG
Ajax 0 United 2
(Young, Hernandez)

THURS 23 EUROPA LEAGUE LAST 32, SECOND LEG
United 1 Ajax 2
(Hernandez)

SUN 26 PREMIER LEAGUE
Norwich 1 United 2
(Scholes, Giggs)

February began and finished with two dramatic league games with **Wayne Rooney** looking particularly sharp in front of goal…

66 When you're 3-0 down at half-time as we were at Chelsea it would have been quite easy to just play the rest of the game and accept defeat, but we always believe, no matter the situation. We worked hard and fought our way back into it and were unlucky not to get three points in the end. Everyone watching the game would have seen that we're not just going to lie down and give in, we'll always fight until the very end. Yes it was two points dropped, but the manner in which we came back galvanised everyone. You saw how motivated all the lads were in the next match against Liverpool – I was delighted to score twice and help us get the win. City may be our main title rivals, but as a Liverpudlian the Liverpool match is still the big one for me because it's a game between the two biggest clubs in England - the rivalry goes back years regardless of where both teams are in the league. We kicked off our Europa League campaign against Ajax and made it through to the last 16 which was pleasing – it was a new challenge for all of us and we wanted to do well. Winning at Norwich was a huge result and to see Ryan [Giggs] pop up with an injury-time winner in his 900th game was amazing. And most importantly it kept us in a good position in the league. 99

FEBRUARY STATS
P5 W3 D1 L1
Scored   10
Conceded   7
Clean sheets   1

Jonny Evans had performed admirably in the absence of Nemanja Vidic and, after an extremely long wait, finally netted his first ever United goal in the win at Wolves...

66 It was a bit of a surreal moment to finally have the chance to celebrate a goal! There had been a lot of banter about me not scoring because it had gone on for so long - a few weeks beforehand someone had shown me a list of United players who had never scored and the number of appearances they'd made and I was about sixth on the list! So from that point of view it was a real relief. It capped a good run of form for both myself and the team in the league, although we were all very disappointed with our performance in both Europa League games against Athletic Club. We were continuing to pick up good results in the league thankfully - going on a run is what we always set out to do especially during the second half of the season and we were going into every match feeling like we were never going to lose. With the end of the season getting closer people were beginning to talk about our desire to win the league being greater than ever because we were competing with City, but in my mind there is always a desire no matter who is challenging. It's not just about City or whoever is challenging, it's about you wanting to create more history at United. You want to be able to look back and be proud of what you've achieved. And we certainly had another title in our sights. 99

2012 March

SUN 4 PREMIER LEAGUE
Tottenham 1 United 3
(Rooney, Young 2)

**THURS 8 EUROPA LEAGUE
LAST 16, FIRST LEG**
United 2 Athletic Club 3
(Rooney 2 (1 pen))

SUN 11 PREMIER LEAGUE
United 2 West Brom 0
(Rooney 2 (1 pen))

**THURS 15 EUROPA LEAGUE
LAST 16, SECOND LEG**
Athletic Club 2 United 1
(Rooney)

SUN 18 PREMIER LEAGUE
Wolves 0 United 5
(Evans, Valencia, Welbeck, Hernandez 2)

MON 26 PREMIER LEAGUE
United 1 Fulham 0
(Rooney)

MARCH STATS
P6 W4 D0 L2
Scored   14
Conceded   6
Clean sheets   3

13

2012

April

MON 2 PREMIER LEAGUE
Blackburn 0 United 2
(Valencia, Young)

SUN 8 PREMIER LEAGUE
United 2 QPR 0
(Rooney (pen) Scholes)

WED 11 PREMIER LEAGUE
Wigan 1 United 0

SUN 15 PREMIER LEAGUE
United 4 Aston Villa 0
(Rooney 2 (1 pen), Welbeck, Nani)

SUN 22 PREMIER LEAGUE
United 4 Everton 4
(Rooney 2, Welbeck, Nani)

MON 30 PREMIER LEAGUE
Manchester City 1 United 0

It was a new experience for **Ashley Young** as the championship race entered the vital closing stages, but unfortunately for United the title pendulum swung back in City's favour…

66 Fighting for the title was everything I expected and more. It was really exciting to be involved especially at the latter stages and we got ourselves into a fantastic position after two vital wins over Blackburn and QPR. A lot of people wrote us off when City were a few points clear with a superior goal difference, but we went about our job in the right way and everyone in the squad made an important contribution. And we did what every other United team seems to do and came strong in the second half of the season. One player who had really come into form was Antonio Valencia. He was immense for us at Blackburn and set us on our way to a big win. I don't think there was a better winger in the league last season. He's like a steam train when he's running at defenders and his delivery is brilliant. As a fellow winger that's something I really admire. We suffered a blip at Wigan but were still in the driving seat in the title race and the 4-0 victory over my old club Villa kept us on course. The month ended on a really disappointing note though with the draw against Everton and the defeat at City. When I came here the manager told me it would be a challenge and that's something I'm always up for. Unfortunately though things were now virtually out of our hands and in City's control. 99

APRIL STATS
P6 W3 D1 L2
Scored 12
Conceded 6
Clean sheets 3

A cruel twist right at the death in the title race left United trophy-less at the end of 2011/12, but **Patrice Evra** still found plenty of cause for optimism…

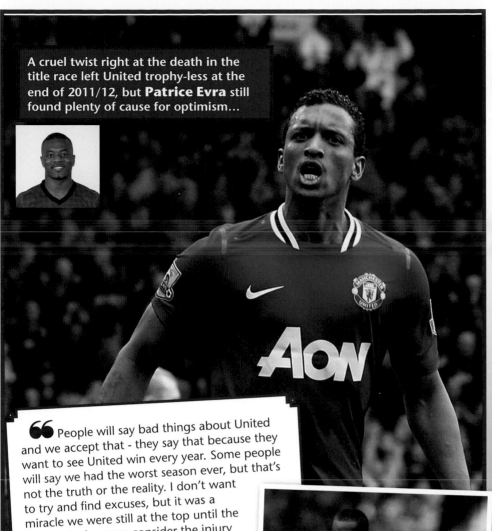

> 66 People will say bad things about United and we accept that - they say that because they want to see United win every year. Some people will say we had the worst season ever, but that's not the truth or the reality. I don't want to try and find excuses, but it was a miracle we were still at the top until the very end when you consider the injury problems we had. We lost our captain for over half of the campaign - take Vincent Kompany out of City's team for most of the season and I want to see if they are still top of the league. We also lost Darren Fletcher and Anderson for long periods and so many other players during the campaign. Yet after all that, we were nine points better off than the season before so we did well, but you have to give credit to City for doing even better. We killed our chances ourselves – we were eight points clear with six games to go and then winning 4-2 against Everton at Old Trafford but drew the game… I didn't think something like that was possible. Every player has to be better next season than last season, even if we weren't as poor as a lot of people said. We realise it's a privilege to play for Manchester United and we'll make sure we work hard in pre-season so we're ready for challenges ahead. 99

2012

May

SUN 6 PREMIER LEAGUE

United 2 Swansea 0
(Scholes, Young)

SUN 13 PREMIER LEAGUE

Sunderland 0 United 1
(Rooney)

MAY STATS
P2 W2 D0 L0
Scored   3
Conceded   0
Clean sheets 2

Manchester United

GOALKEEPERS

1. David De Gea

Born: 7 November 1990; Madrid, Spain

Previous clubs: Atletico Madrid

Joined United: 1 July 2011

United debut: 7 August 2011 vs Manchester City (N), Community Shield

International team: Spain (youth)

Replacing a goalkeeper of Edwin van der Sar's calibre is near-impossible, but in David De Gea, Sir Alex Ferguson signed a young custodian with the skills to have a similar impact to the veteran Dutchman. Still only a fledgling talent, Spanish under-21 stopper David can boast stunning reflexes, nonchalant distribution and terrific temperament. After a tough start to life in England, De Gea's form in the second half of his maiden Reds campaign suggested that a bright future lies in store for United's number one..

13. Anders Lindegaard

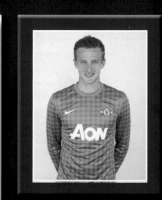

Born: 13 April 1984; Dyrup, Denmark

Previous clubs: Odense Boldklub, Kolding FC (loan), Aalesunds FK

Joined United: 4 January 2011

United debut: 29 January 2011 vs Southampton (A), FA Cup

International team: Denmark

A mid-season arrival during the 2010/11 campaign, Danish international stopper Anders Lindegaard made a seamless adaptation to life at Old Trafford. A modern goalkeeper is expected to exceed with the ball at his feet, and Anders is one of the very best in that field. With that attribute, allied to Lindegaard's superb shot-stopping, communication and command of his penalty area, Sir Alex Ferguson is now extremely well-stocked for senior goalkeepers.

50. Sam Johnstone

Born: 25 March 1993; Preston

Previous clubs: Trainee, Oldham (loan), Scunthorpe (loan)

Joined United: 1 July 2009

United debut: N/A

International team: England (youth)

A fixture throughout England's youth ranks, Sam Johnstone is a highly-rated young goalkeeper with a bright future. The Preston-born stopper has developed a mountainous physique and plays with a growing confidence which makes him an imposing presence in the United goal. As well as starring for the Reds' Reserves – saving three penalties in one shootout to earn them the national title - he has sampled life in competitive football with loan stints at Oldham and Scunthorpe and also received the invaluable experience of joining Sir Alex Ferguson's squad in their two most recent pre-season tours.

DEFENDERS

2. Rafael da Silva

Born: 9 July 1990; Rio de Janeiro, Brazil

Previous club: Fluminense

Joined United: 1 July 2008

United debut: 17 August 2008 vs Newcastle (H), Premier League

International team: Brazil

It took just 90 minutes in a pre-season friendly at Peterborough to convince Sir Alex Ferguson that Rafael da Silva was ready for first team action at United. The bombarding Brazilian duly took his chance, too. His pace and proactivity occasionally betrayed his attacking instincts as a product of Samba football, but he increasingly demonstrated that he has the character and skill to cope with high-pressure occasions and big-name opponents.

3. Patrice Evra

Born: 15 May 1981; Dakar, Senegal

Previous clubs: Masala, Monza, Monaco

Joined United: 10 January 2006

United debut: 14 January 2006 vs Manchester City (A), Premier League

International team: France

Patrice Evra's first full season at Old Trafford coincided with the Premier League title's return, and the French left-back has picked up silverware galore ever since. A bombarding presence on the Reds' left flank, he established himself as one of the finest full-backs around after arriving from Monaco, and his stance within the United squad was underlined when he captained the Reds in the absence of Nemanja Vidic during the 2011/12 campaign.

4. Phil Jones

Born: 21 February 1992; Preston

Previous clubs: Blackburn Rovers

Joined United: 1 July 2011

United debut: 7 August 2011 vs Manchester City (N), Community Shield

International team: England

One of the hottest young talents in English football, Phil Jones was coveted by most of the Barclays Premier League's top clubs before United swooped to snap him up from Blackburn Rovers. His first season at Old Trafford didn't disappoint. As a marauding centre-back or full-back with total confidence in his ability on the ball, he quickly established himself as a fans' favourite, and he even chipped in with a couple of goals during rare outings as a central midfielder.

5. Rio Ferdinand

Born: 7 November 1978; Peckham

Previous clubs: West Ham, Bournemouth (loan), Leeds United

Joined United: 22 July 2002

United debut: 27 August 2002 vs Zalaegerszeg (H), UEFA Champions League

International team: England

Having celebrated a decade as a mainstay of the Reds' backline, Rio Ferdinand has long since established himself as one of the finest defenders in the club's history. A vocal organiser and leader at the back, his trademark cool head under the fiercest pressure and intelligent use of the ball has been key to United's successes. With such an outstanding football brain and oodles of experience, Rio has the wherewithal to feature prominently at Old Trafford for years to come.

6. Jonny Evans

Born: 2 January 1998; Belfast, Northern Ireland

Previous clubs: Trainee, Royal Antwerp (loan), Sunderland (loan)

Joined United: 1 July 2004

United debut: 26 September 2007 vs Coventry City (H), League Cup

International team: Northern Ireland

Northern Irish international Jonny Evans has been a highly-rated prospect among United's coaching staff for a number of years, and his first full season at senior level in 2008/09 bore out their faith. Two steady campaigns followed, but in 2011/12 Jonny announced himself in Nemanja Vidic's absence. Now a powerful, proactive defender who reads the game superbly, Jonny has realised his potential to become one of the finest centre-backs in the Premier League.

12. Chris Smalling

Born: 22 November 1989; Greenwich

Previous clubs: Maidstone United, Fulham

Joined United: 7 July 2010

United debut: 8 August 2010 vs Chelsea (N), Community Shield

International team: England

Despite completing a mind-blowingly quick rise to prominence, going from non-league Maidstone to United in the space of two years, Chris Smalling quickly demonstrated that he was born to play on the biggest stage. Now a fully-fledged England international, the tall, imposing defender brings intelligence and ice-cool temperament to the Reds' backline, whether he's fielded centrally or as a rampaging right-back, and he looks set to become a mainstay of the United defence for years to come.

DEFENDERS

15. Nemanja Vidic

Born: 21 October 1981; Uzice, Serbia

Previous clubs: Red Star Belgrade, Spartak Moscow

Joined United: 5 January 2006

United debut: 25 January 2006 vs Blackburn Rovers (H), League Cup

International team: Serbia (retired)

The no-nonsense, full-blooded playing style of Nemanja Vidic not only instantly endeared him to United supporters, it also convinced Sir Alex Ferguson that he was worthy of becoming club captain. The Serbian international spent years as half of arguably the world's finest central defensive partnership with Rio Ferdinand and established himself as one of the most important names on the Reds' teamsheet. Though he missed much of 2011/12 through a serious knee injury, his return to fitness marks a huge boost for United.

31. Scott Wootton

Born: 12 September 1991; Birkenhead

Previous clubs: Liverpool, Tranmere Rovers (loan), Peterborough (loan), Nottingham Forest (loan)

Joined United: 1 July 2007

United debut: N/A

International team: England (youth)

Scott Wootton is a strong and cultured central defender who has risen to the fringe of United's first team squad after joining the Reds' Academy in 2007. The youngster made the rare switch from Liverpool's youth system and quickly validated his move with a series of impressive displays in United's under-18s and Reserves. He further benefited from loan spells with Tranmere Rovers, Peterborough and Nottingham Forest, and his game developed sufficiently to warrant inclusion in the Reds' 2012/13 pre-season tour, where he also caught the eye.

MIDFIELDERS

7. Antonio Valencia

Born: 4 August 1985; Lago Agrio, Ecuador

Previous clubs: El Nacional, Villarreal, Wigan

Joined United: 30 June 2009

United debut: 9 August 2009 v Chelsea (N), Community Shield

International team: Ecuador

There are few defenders around who can cope with Antonio Valencia in full flight. Built like a tank with afterburners, the fast, powerful Ecuadorian winger is one of the Reds' most devastating attacking weapons and is a firm fans' favourite. Antonio made a seamless transition to life at Old Trafford after joining from Wigan in 2009 and, although he has overcome two serious injuries in the subsequent years, his value was underlined when he swept the board at United's 2011/12 season awards.

8. Anderson

Born: 13 April 1988; Porto Alegre, Brazil

Previous clubs: Gremio, FC Porto

Joined United: 1 July 2007

United debut: 1 September 2007 vs Sunderland (H), Premier League

International team: Brazil

An all-action midfielder with the rare gift of being able to carry the ball and meander his way through packed areas, Anderson brings character and panache to Sir Alex Ferguson's squad. After his arrival from Porto in 2007, the Brazilian international announced himself as a newcomer to watch after a series of impressive displays against more illustrious opponents, and he is never fazed by reputations. Though injuries have taken their toll on Anderson's United career to date, he remains a valuable wild card for any midfield battle.

11. Ryan Giggs

Born: 29 November 1973; Cardiff, Wales

Previous clubs: Trainee

Joined United: 9 July 1990

United debut: 2 March 1991 vs Everton (H), First Division

International team: Wales (retired)

Superlatives have long since run dry for Ryan Giggs. The bare facts are that he is United's all-time record appearance-maker with over 900 outings for the club, and he is the most successful player in the history of English football after collecting a spate of medals in domestic and European football. Still an influential presence, be it on the left flank or in a central role, Ryan is a footballing phenomenon and one of the game's true legends.

MIDFIELDERS

16. Michael Carrick

Born: 29 July 1981; Wallsend

Previous clubs: West Ham, Swindon (loan), Birmingham (loan), Tottenham Hotspur

Joined United: 31 July 2006

United debut: 23 August 2006 vs Charlton Athletic (A), Premier League

International team: England

As a deep-lying midfielder armed with an astute range of passing with either foot, Michael Carrick quietly damages United's opponents from a position of no apparent threat. Having played alongside and learned from Paul Scholes since his 2006 arrival from Tottenham, Carrick has mastered the art of holding possession and patiently picking the right pass. While the role may not bring the same plaudits as Wayne Rooney's goalscoring or Antonio Valencia's wingplay, Carrick's importance to the team is utterly vital.

17. Nani

Born: 17 November 1986; Praia, Cape Verde

Previous club: Sporting Lisbon

Joined United: 1 July 2007

United debut: 5 August 2007 vs Chelsea (N), Community Shield

International team: Portugal

Nani's United career began with the 2007/08 Double, and ever since the young Portuguese winger has grown and matured into an important part of the Reds' success. Few players in the game are as competently two-footed as Nani, whose trickery is capable of baffling opposing defenders, while his powerful shooting can outwit goalkeepers from long range. In an increasingly defensive sport, Nani's unpredictability makes him one of modern football's most engaging entertainers.

18. Ashley Young

Born: 9 July 1985; Stevenage

Previous clubs: Watford, Aston Villa

Joined United: 1 July 2011

United debut: 7 August 2011 vs Manchester City (N), Community Shield

International team: England

After regularly turning in outstanding performances against United, Ashley Young convinced Sir Alex Ferguson to bring him to Old Trafford in 2011, and the England international quickly slotted into the Reds' style of play. A fast, tricky right-footer who usually operates on the left wing, Young is a thorn in any full-back's side. His versatility and added ability to operate in a central role behind a striker makes him an invaluable addition to the Reds' fluid attack, and his first season at United promises much for the future.

22. Paul Scholes

Born: 16 November 1974; Salford

Previous Clubs: Trainee

Joined United: 8 July 1991

United Debut: 21 September 1994 v Port Vale (A), League Cup

International Team: England (retired)

Now in his second stint as a Red after reversing his 2011 retirement, Paul Scholes' influence remains intact. Part of the new wave of talent that ushered in Beckham, Giggs, Butt and the Nevilles in the mid-1990s, the modest midfielder scored twice on his debut at Port Vale and has never looked back. A player who has the ability to control a game in the simplest of fashions, he also has a deadly eye for goal both inside and outside the box and is indisputably one of the finest talents in United's history.

23. Tom Cleverley

Born: 12 August 1989; Basingstoke

Previous clubs: Trainee, Leicester City (loan), Watford (loan), Wigan (loan)

Joined United: 1 July 2005

United debut: 7 August 2011 vs Manchester City (N), Community Shield

International team: England

Patience is a virtue which Tom Cleverley fortunately possesses. The gifted young midfielder was a late developer physically as he rose through the United ranks, and he suffered from a string of serious injuries during his Academy education and three subsequent senior loan spells. After breaking into the United first team in 2011/12 and dictating the Reds' scorching start to the season, another injury set him back, but Sir Alex Ferguson's assertion that he is potentially the best midfielder in Britain indicates that Cleverley's Old Trafford future is extremely bright.

24. Darren Fletcher

Born: 1 February 1984; Edinburgh, Scotland

Previous clubs: Trainee

Joined United: 3 July 2000

United debut: 12 March 2003 vs FC Basel (H), Champions League

International team: Scotland

Another product of the United Academy, Darren Fletcher has been one of the most reliable midfielders in the Reds' recent history. His non-stop effort and intelligent reading of the game marked him out as an ideal big-game player, and his reward has been a spate of honours in almost a decade of first-team football. His recent seasons have been affected by illness, however, and United's coaching and medical teams have given the Scotland international as much time as he needs to recover, such is his importance to the cause.

MIDFIELDER

45. Davide Petrucci

Born: 5 October 1991; Rome, Italy

Previous club: AS Roma

Joined United: 5 March 2009

International team: Italy (youth)

A gifted young playmaker, Davide Petrucci has demonstrated admirable patience during his short United career to date. The Italian midfielder was beset with injury issues during his first couple of seasons after arriving from Roma, but he was able to showcase his unquestioned talent even during fleeting glimpses of him on the field. Blessed with a terrific array of passing and a soothing serenity in possession of the ball, Petrucci brings class to the midfield minefield, and he appeared completely at home at senior level when he partook in the Reds' 2012/13 pre-season tour. Having overcome the hindrances of his early days at United and been entrusted with the responsibility of captaining the Reds' Reserves under Warren Joyce, the gifted young Italian is now poised to take his game to the next level.

STRIKERS

10. Wayne Rooney

Born: 24 October 1985; Liverpool

Previous club: Everton

Joined United: 31 August 2004

United debut: 28 September 2004 vs Fenerbahce (H), Champions League

International team: England

The jewel in United's crown. Ever since he bagged a hat-trick on his Reds debut – only the second player to achieve such a feat – Wayne Rooney has led the line with distinction at Old Trafford. The England star has punctuated his career with spectacular goals, not least his now-legendary overhead kick against Manchester City, but moreover has become a prolific scorer. Rooney drops deep to dictate play and has also played on either flank or in midfield, such is his versatility and ability, and he remains the Reds' deadliest attacker.

14. Javier Hernandez

Born: 1 June 1988; Guadalajara, Mexico

Previous Clubs: Chivas de Guadalajara

Joined United: 1 July 2010

United debut: 6 August 2010 vs Chelsea (N), Community Shield

International team: Mexico

Few signings have had the immediate impact of Chicharito. The little Mexican was an unknown quantity in English and European football when he arrived at Old Trafford in 2010, but an incredible first season with the Reds established him as one of the deadliest poachers around. Blessed with incredible pace, unfathomable movement and unerring finishing, Chicharito soon endeared himself to United supporters with a hefty goals return and his non-stop endeavour. Despite an injury-hit second season, he is a key member of the Reds' attack.

19. Danny Welbeck

Born: 26 November 1990; Manchester

Previous clubs: Trainee, Preston North End (loan), Sunderland (loan)

Joined United: 1 July 2007

United debut: 23 September 2008 vs Middlesbrough (H), League Cup

International team: England

The first home-reared striker to come through the United ranks since Mark Hughes, Danny Welbeck is on track to becoming a star. The Longsight goal-getter benefited from a season-long loan at Sunderland in 2010/11 and returned to Old Trafford ready to become a key member of Sir Alex Ferguson's attacking arsenal. Full of running and blessed with terrific skill and ball retention, Danny is the local lad made good, and a potential fixture in the United and England forward line for years to come.

27. Federico Macheda

Born: 22 August 1991; Rome, Italy

Previous club: Lazio, Sampdoria (loan) QPR (loan)

Joined United: 1 September 2007

United debut: 5 April 2009 vs Aston Villa (H), Premier League

International team: Italy (youth)

United's youngest goalscorer in the Premier League era, Kiko Macheda enjoyed an unforgettable start to life in senior football with a debut winner against Aston Villa. The Italian striker popped up with further important goals for the Reds, but embarked on loan deals with Sampdoria and Queens Park Rangers in search of more regular action. It proved hard to come by, but Sir Alex Ferguson remains convinced of Macheda's abilities and will be keen to lean on his poacher's instinct in the future.

33. Bebe

Born: 12 July 1990; Agualva-Cacem, Portugal

Previous clubs: Estrela Amadora, Vitoria de Guimaraes

Joined United: 4 August 2010

United debut: 22 September 2010 v Scunthorpe (A), Carling Cup

International: Portugal (youth)

Bebe's rise from the third tier of Portuguese football to United in the space of just six weeks has been likened to a fairytale story. The previously unknown attacker was signed by Sir Alex Ferguson on the recommendation of United's Portuguese scout, and he bagged a pair of senior goals in his maiden campaign at Old Trafford. His second season was earmarked for a loan spell at Besiktas, only for a serious knee injury to heavily disrupt his time in Turkey. He subsequently returned to Old Trafford, and the next chapter in his fascinating tale is yet to be written.

NEW ARRIVALS

Sir Alex Ferguson used the summer 2012 transfer window to strengthen his squad and, as ever, demonstrated that he has a keen eye for burgeoning talents...

20. Robin van Persie

Born: 6 August 1983; Rotterdam, Netherlands

Position: Striker

Previous clubs: Feyenoord, Arsenal

Joined United: 17 August 2012

International team: Netherlands

United's capture of Arsenal skipper and talisman Robin van Persie stunned football, with the Dutchman adding further menace and class to an already imposing forward line. Having announced his decision to leave the Emirates Stadium, the striker quickly decided that he only wanted to move to Old Trafford. "Manchester United breathes football," he said. "When I have to make hard decisions, I always listen to little boy inside me and what he wants. That little boy was screaming for United." The Dutchman's decision to join the Reds over other suitors, such as Manchester City and Juventus, provided a huge boost for all those associated with the club, with Wayne Rooney admitting: "It's great for the players and the fans to sign a player of Robin's quality."

21. Angelo Henriquez

Born: 13 April 1994; Santiago, Chile

Position: Striker

Previous club: Universidad de Chile

Joined United: 31 August 2012

International team: Chile (youth)

Having been dubbed 'the Chilean Ruud van Nistelrooy', Angelo Henriquez arrived at Old Trafford with huge promise and a growing reputation in his home country. The striker caught United's attention in his early teens, and had been set to move to Old Trafford in the summer of 2013, before interest from other clubs provoked his early capture. Henriquez has repeatedly demonstrated his penalty area prowess with Chile's youth teams and with Universidad de Chile, and his arrival in England is an exciting coup for Sir Alex Ferguson.

25. Nick Powell

Born: 23 March 1994; Crewe

Position: Midfielder/striker

Previous club: Crewe Alexandra

Joined United: 1 July 2012

International team: England (youth)

Very few teenagers garner as much attention as Nick Powell, but the England youth international has long-since been ahead of his time. On his way up through the Crewe Alexandra ranks, he debuted in under-18s football at just 15 and was still only 16 when he made his competitive senior debut. His breakthrough campaign came in 2011/12, as he played an integral part in the Railwaymen's promotion to League One, bagging a scorching opener in their play-off final victory and scoring 16 times in 45 appearances. The Reds have signed a rare talent, according to Crewe director of youth football, Dario Gradi, who labelled Powell: 'a match winner.'

26. Shinji Kagawa

Born: 17 March 1989; Kobe, Japan

Position: Attacking midfielder

Previous clubs: FC Miyagi Barcelona, Cerezo Osaka, Borussia Dortmund

Joined United: 1 July 2012

International team: Japan

From the Japanese second division to Old Trafford in the space of just two years, Shinji Kagawa's route to the top has been on fast forward since he was spotted by Borussia Dortmund in 2010. The skilful, pacey attacking midfielder, who can operate in central positions or on either flank, played a key part in Dortmund's back-to-back Bundesliga triumph, and was quickly earmarked by Sir Alex Ferguson as a United player in-waiting. "Shinji is an exciting young midfielder with great skill, vision and a good eye for goal," said the United manager. "I am delighted he has chosen to come here. I believe he will make an impact upon the team very quickly as he is suited to United's style of play."

28. Alexander Büttner

Born: 11 February 1989; Doetinchem, Netherlands

Position: Left-back

Previous clubs: Ajax, Vitesse Arnhem

Joined United: 21 August 2012

International team: Netherlands (youth)

The Reds' defence was bolstered by the arrival of Dutch defender Alexander Büttner, who arrived from Vitesse Arnhem on a five-year contract shortly after the start of the 2012/13 season. The full-back, who was part of Holland's preliminary squad for Euro 2012, was labelled by Sir Alex Ferguson as: "One of the best young left-backs in Europe." The manager added: "We're delighted to sign him. He's someone we've been watching for a while now. He gives us some really exciting options in that position."

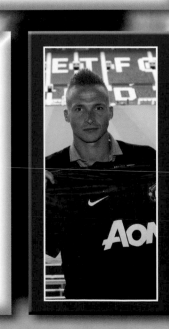

A decade in Red

Rio Ferdinand arrived at Manchester United in the summer of 2002 as the world's most expensive defender. A decade on, the veteran stopper looks back on the snapshots of some of his most unforgettable highlights with the Reds...

2002

Signing for United was one of the best days of my life – and what a great suit. I stand by that suit, even today!

One of my best moments: winning the league and my first trophy in football. Just to get that feeling of winning was amazing, and it's something that will never leave me.

2003

2006

> When you sign for this club, you dream of scoring at the Stretford End, but to do it in the last minute against Liverpool was amazing. If you could bottle that emotion, you'd be minted!

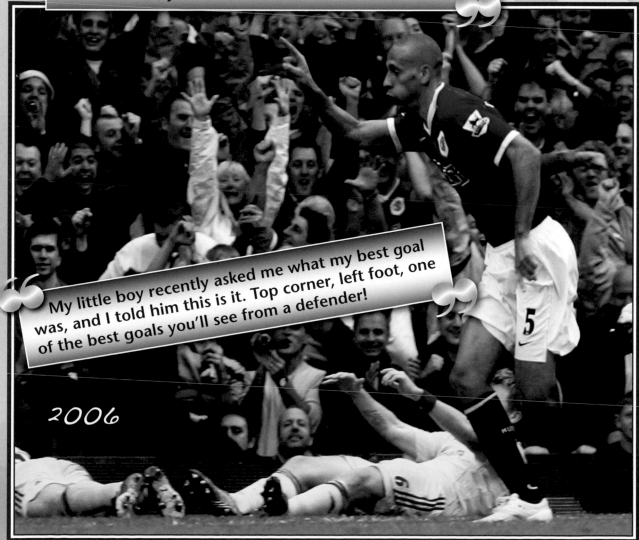

> My little boy recently asked me what my best goal was, and I told him this is it. Top corner, left foot, one of the best goals you'll see from a defender!

2006

2007

What a great night. You think you'll never be able to win the Champions League, it's the hardest tournament to win, but to do it and be captain on the night left me speechless.

We'd been out celebrating winning the league the night before, and we just went crazy, spraying each other with champagne. This is what it's about. The emotion of those moments is great.

2008

2008

We were crowned the champions of the world. Not many people in their lives will be able to say they're a world champion, and we were on that night.

2011

We just needed a point to win the league and we did that at Blackburn that day. I'm more interested in Wazza's barnet here, actually. He's made a massive improvement since then!

2012

A disappointing night. Barcelona were better than us. When we scored I thought there was a chance, but that man Messi was the difference. No-one's going to face them at that level again.

2011

Giggsy's last minute goal at Norwich was an unbelievable moment in terms of celebrating with the fans. Unbelievable to win it at the last minute, but typical United to do it in such dramatic fashion.

VERY SUPERSTITIOUS

Preparation for games might be largely conducted on the training field, but as a number of the players explain here, there are also a host of special rituals which the Reds incorporate into their individual pre-match routines...

❝I've got quite a few superstitions that I have to follow before kick-off. This sounds really stupid... but it depends on whether we're home or away. The fixtures list always has United on the left when we're at home and on the right when we're away. So if we're away one weekend I'll put my right sock on first because it will say the away team v United. And then the next week when we're at Old Trafford, I'll put my left sock on because we'll be on the left as the fixture is listed. Also, when I walk onto the pitch, I'll take the first step across the white line with the foot that corresponds to whether we're home or away. This will sound proper over-the-top, but you know when you go to a hotel room and there are two towels hanging down? When I was on international duty last season, I picked the towel on the left because we were at home against Spain. I know it's weird but I can't help myself. Nobody knew about all this so nobody had ever noticed but I guess the secret's out now!❞

Phil Jones

❝I have a lot of rituals! They start the night before a game. I always have a shave and then I do my homework and look at who we're playing against and how their strikers play.

As the day progresses I eat the same things every time - porridge and pasta. I try and maintain the same sleep patterns too. I try and sleep especially well for the two nights before the game. The way I put on my outfit is important too... I always put on my right shin-pad before the left, as well as the tape on my shin-pad. I wrap the tape four times around my leg at the bottom and twice around my leg at the top. I put my right glove on before the left and if anything happens out of order, I start again from scratch. I used to think having all these routines was a superstitious thing, but as I've grown older I feel like it's more about getting in the right zone. If I walk onto the pitch after doing all those things correctly then I know I'm in the right place. It helps me focus. Focus is a big part of being a goalkeeper. The game is a state of mind for a goalkeeper. You can have a lot of physical attributes but if your mind isn't right you're not going to make it.❞

Anders Lindegaard

66 My routine consists of having a pre-match meal and then when we're on the way to the stadium I'll listen to music on my headphones. We get to the stadium, have a meeting, and then Patrice [Evra] will put his iPod on in the dressing room. In terms of superstitions, I'll stretch my socks a little bit and I'll put whichever one's longest on my right foot. I always do my left boot up first before my right but that's about it. 99

Chris Smalling

66Music has always been a big part of my life. It's from my dad. In Senegal we love music, we love to dance. I feel so blessed to be the team DJ. I have about 16,000 on my iPod and before each game I go through the playlist in my room and try to find a good mix of songs that everyone will like.99

Patrice Evra

66My pre-match ritual is to go into the physio's room after the warm-up and pray - that's about it really. I'm quite relaxed. I listen to a bit of music - I have my own iPod so I don't really listen to what Patrice puts on although I must say he does put on some decent stuff now and again! 99

Wayne Rooney

66As soon as I walk out on to the pitch and hit the white line I always jump. I've no idea where it came from, it's just a superstition and something I've always done. I also like to put water on my face before the game and at half-time. I've done all sorts of other things like putting my strapping on a certain foot, in a certain way at a certain time, and I used to wear a ring on my little finger for good luck. But the jumping thing has always stayed with me.99

Rio Ferdinand

Milestone Man

Ryan Giggs has played for Manchester United over 900 times. So, just how does the veteran Welshman still cut it at the highest level?

Ability

First and foremost, Ryan's skills as a footballer have fuelled his career. He's won more medals than any other player in the history of English football; you don't manage that without incredible ability. "When you watch Ryan Giggs, you're watching greatness," insists former team-mate Gary Neville. "He can sit in the centre of midfield and dictate and control the tempo of the match, provide passes that no-one else can provide, provide moments of quality at the right moment that nobody else can deliver. He's an incredible player who just defeats time."

> 66 He can sit in the centre of midfield and dictate and control the tempo of the match. 99
>
> Gary Neville

In his younger days, Giggs regularly succumbed to hamstring injuries. He investigated and mastered the problem with the help of regular yoga sessions, and now he has learned his body's limits and how to utilise them. "Ryan is the perfect football athlete," says United's head of fitness and conditioning, Tony Strudwick. "He has a physical capacity that not many athletes possess. He uses less energy per stride, so he's a smoother, more efficient athlete. That allows him to get through the number of games he has, as does the way he eats and lives. He's an ideal professional."

Mentality

Of course, no player could keep putting their body through the rigours of over 20 years of professional football without the equivalent mental strength, and Strudwick says Ryan can call upon an incredible sense of calm and perspective. "What differentiates Ryan from a lot of athletes is his mental strength," adds the fitness guru. "He is fazed by nothing. His mental strength, particularly at key moments of games, can be match-winning for us. That makes him the go-to guy when we're under pressure."

> **His mental strength, particularly at key moments of games, can be match-winning for us.**
>
> Tony Strudwick

Adaptability

Ryan became United's record appearance-maker in the 2008 Champions League final victory over Chelsea, and has completed another century and a half of games ever since. Sir Alex Ferguson puts the Giggs' longevity down to his ability to adapt his style of play with age. "It is amazing," admits Sir Alex. "His use of the ball has got better with age. Changing his position to play in a more central area has given a different aspect to his game. We always remember what Ryan was famous for: running at full-backs with great balance and speed. Today it is a different Ryan Giggs. He has looked at his game a different way."

Despite winning almost every major honour in club football with United, Ryan's sights are always set on what he can achieve in the future, and that tunnel vision continues to keep him going strong. "All I've ever wanted to do is play for United and I've been lucky enough to do that for 20 years," says the man himself. "It's great to know I'm still contributing to the team's success and this club is all about what we do next and I'm really pleased I can be part of that."

> 66 All I've ever wanted to do is play for United and I've been lucky enough to do that for 20 years 99
> **Ryan Giggs**

PRACTICE
makes Perfect

PRIZE GUYS

A number of Reds were presented with a host of prestigious personal accolades for their performances on the pitch, not just last season, but during 20 campaigns of the Premier League era...

Victorious Valencia

Antonio made a clean sweep of the awards at the club's annual Player of the Year ceremony...

It was arguably one of the most open races for many years when it came to the fans' and players' choices for Player of the Year for 2011/12, as well as Goal of the Season. But, in the end, supporters and squad members alike were in full agreement that Antonio Valencia deserved to scoop all three prizes. Never one to exude emotion, the Ecuadorian remained as calm and assured as he is on the pitch when he learned of his triple triumph at a gala dinner with his team-mates at Old Trafford, though he was understandably delighted and proud by the recognition.

"I am very happy to receive all three awards and I will take a lot of heart from this," he said during his acceptance speech. "There should be 20 of these awards because all of my team-mates deserve one. I'd like to thank them and my fans at home in Ecuador and Manchester United fans everywhere."

Sir Alex was quick to heap praise on the shy winger, adding: "The form he produced last season after coming back from injury was amazing. He's a great professional and he has the qualities we love in our game. I think that's why the other players and the fans gave him both of the main awards."

Goal of the Season   Valencia v Blackburn (a), 2 April 2012

In a game of high importance in the title race, United were kept at bay by a dogged Blackburn side for 81 minutes before Valencia finally broke the deadlock with a moment of magic, and sheer power, to set the Reds on their way to vital victory.

After picking the ball up on the right wing, he made a beeline for the home side's box where, from just inside it, he unleashed a piledriver which flew across goal and past Rovers keeper Paul Robinson into the far corner to spark delirium in the away end, and also a rare outbreak of emotion from the man himself.

Valencia wasn't the only winner at the awards dinner – Michael Keane was named the Denzil Haroun Reserve Player of the Year by fans after an excellent campaign at the heart of United's title-winning defence, while Norwegian midfielder Mats Daehli was presented with the Jimmy Murphy Young Player of the Year prize at the end of an impressive maiden season in the club's under-18s side.

Michael Keane 2011/12 Reserves stats:
27 appearances 5 goals

Mats Daehli 2011/12 Academy stats:
22 appearances 4 goals

> I was surprised, but really pleased to win the award. It's great to know that it's been voted for by the fans because they come to watch us and follow us throughout the season.
> **Michael Keane**

> I'm very proud to win the award and pleased that the season went well for us. Everyone here has taken great care of me, I've settled in well and hopefully that will continue.
> **Mats Daehli**

20 seasons of the Premier League

At the end of the 2011/12 campaign, the greatest players, managers and moments from the last 20 years of the Premier League were honoured and, as expected, a number of Reds featured in the winners' list…

BEST MATCH
United 4-3 Manchester City
20 September 2009

BEST MANAGER
Sir Alex Freguson

BEST PLAYER
Ryan Giggs

BEST GOAL (above)
Wayne Rooney
Manchester City 12 February 2011

BEST GOAL CELEBRATION (left)
Eric Cantona United v Sunderland
21 December 1996

Fantasy Teams Fans' XI

| Peter Schmeichel | Gary Neville | Tony Adams | Nemanja Vidic | Ashley Cole | Cristiano Ronaldo | Paul Scholes | Steven Gerrard | Ryan Giggs | Thierry Henry | Alan Shearer |

Fantasy Teams Experts' XI

| Peter Schmeichel | Gary Neville | Tony Adams | Rio Ferdinand | Ashley Cole | Cristiano Ronaldo | Paul Scholes | Roy Keane | Ryan Giggs | Thierry Henry | Alan Shearer |

: AWAY FROM HOME :

Want to know what the lads get up to in preparation for a European away match? Here, we take you behind the scenes on a typical trip to the Continent...

09:00 Airport check-in

The players arrive at Manchester Airport for their morning flight, usually around 10am, which also includes directors, coaching staff, commercial and media staff and a host of club legends, some of whom are now United ambassadors.

The team relax in the airport lounge before boarding the flight, during which computer games, music and books are the order of the day. On arrival at their destination, the players are usually greeted by a large number of local fans and media

13:00 Lunch

After a spot of lunch immediately on arrival at the team hotel, the players return to their rooms to rest before the evening training session.
Those who need treatment will make a visit to the specially created medical room at the hotel. There is also a designated kit room where the training and match kit, including boots, is stored.

17:00 Pre-match press conference

Around 5pm local time Sir Alex, a chosen player and the club's communications and media teams are driven to the opposition team's stadium for the pre-match press conference where the manager and player address the gathered press pack. Sometimes there is also time for a quick look around the stadium.

18:30 Training

The rest of the squad follow soon after for a training session at the stadium, the first 15 minutes of which are open to the media

On occasion, some familiar faces pop by to catch up with the boss and former team-mates. And some famous faces have also been known to stop in at the team HQ – here Sir Alex, Rio and Wayne chat to music star P Diddy.

11:00 Matchday – preparation

The players, who always keep their watches and clocks set to British time while they are away so there is no upset to their pre-match routine, usually have breakfast between 8 and 9am. The squad take part in a brief stretching session with fitness coach Tony Strudwick before attending a team meeting where the players are shown videos of the opposition and informed about particular players and tactics.

On most trips, Sir Alex and his men will go for a short stroll around the city, often to the delight of the excited locals.

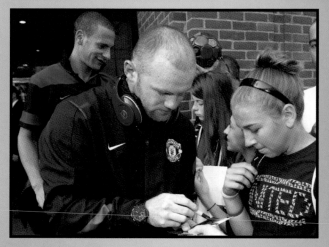

13:00 Pre-match time

Lunch is followed by an afternoon of relaxation for the players, most of whom go for a sleep in their rooms. Around four hours before kick-off, the players return to their private dining room for their pre-match meal before boarding the team coach which is given a police escort to the stadium.

19:45 Kick-off

Come kick-off the lads get down to business on the pitch and are always well supported by the loyal travelling Red army.

After the match, Sir Alex answers questions at the post-match press conference, while the players – from both teams - are quizzed by the media in an area known as the mixed zone.

The Reds have been known to stay over an extra night after a European game, but on most occasions the squad head straight for the airport to catch a late flight home in order to begin preparations at Carrington for their next game.

45

Red inspiration

See what Sir Alex and the players do away from the pitch to help aid The MU Foundation's work

Being a Manchester United player is not just about playing entertaining football and winning trophies, the squad also spend as much time as they're able between training and matches to lend their support to a number of charitable and community causes via the Manchester United Foundation.

The Foundation is the charity arm of the club and was set up in 2006. It uses the power of football and the passion for United to help educate, motivate and inspire future generations to build better communities for all in the North West and around the world.

By delivering football coaching, skills training, personal development and life-changing experiences the Foundation helps provide young people with opportunities to change their lives for the better and this is something that the players get involved in whenever they can.

1. Ryan Giggs meets local AIDS-affected children in Guangzhou, China in 2007, playing games with the youngsters as part of the Foundation's 'United for Unicef' partnership.

2. United defenders past and present – Gary Pallister, Patrice Evra and Nemanja Vidic – share a joke at the Foundation's annual 'Lunch with Legends' event.

3. Ex-Red Dwight Yorke and television presenter Tim Lovejoy go head-to-head during the 2010 United Relief fundraising match at Old Trafford.

4. Sir Bobby Charlton presents Wayne Rooney with his trophy for winning the 2012 Foundation Golf Day tournament at Dunham Forest Golf and Country Club.

5. Danny Welbeck, Nani and Phil Jones spread Christmas cheer with their annual visit to the Royal Manchester Children's Hospital.

6. Treble winner Denis Irwin and former United striker Andy Ritchie headed a fundraising trek through the Sahara Desert in 2009.

7. Sir Alex Ferguson and Ben Amos (pictured centre) meet orphans and vulnerable children helped by the UNICEF-supported 'Isibindi' project in Durban, South Africa in 2012.

8. First-team coach Rene Meulensteen gives the players orders ahead of a fan-attended open training session at Old Trafford in 2011.

ONES TO WATCH

We shine the spotlight on five talented youngsters from within the Reds' Reserves and Academy sides...

Name: Mats Daehli
Birthdate: 02 March 1995

Birthplace: Oslo, Norway
Position: Midfielder

Diminutive playmaker Mats Daehli is one of the most exciting young talents to grace the Reds' youth system in recent years. The skilful little Norwegian is every inch a modern string-puller who excels with the ball at his feet in tight situations, while his vision and range of passing make him an invaluable attacking weapon. His eye-catching form for Paul McGuinness' under-18s earned him the Jimmy Murphy Young Player of the Year award in 2011/12, and the future appears very bright for the highly-rated youngster, who has long since appeared ready to make the regular leap to Reserves level football.

Name: James Wilson
Birthdate: 01 December 1995

Birthplace: Biddulph
Position: Forward

Exciting young striker James Wilson has often played ahead of his age group, and his form with the Reds' under-18s looks likely to prolong that trend over the coming seasons. Called up to England Schoolboys when still performing at under-15 level, the skilful forward was scouted by United at just seven years of age. Though versatile enough to operate on the left wing, Wilson is at his most effective in central areas, where his composure and poacher's instinct really come to the fore. Having already made his Reserves bow at just 16, the teenager's fast-track to prominence continues to make compelling viewing.

Name: Tyler Blackett

Birthdate: 02 April 1994

Birthplace: Manchester
Position: Defender

Manchester-born defender Tyler Blackett has been with United since he was eight years old, progressing right through the ranks at the club and playing an integral part in the Reds' 2011 FA Youth Cup triumph. He was also included in the first team squad for United's 2012 pre-season tour of South Africa and China and made his first senior appearance in the Reds' opening game. A tall, powerful defender who can operate at centre-back or left-back, Tyler is extremely adept at bombarding forward down the left flank, and has even been used as a winger in the past. Given his added threat from set-pieces, the England youth international is expected to take the step up to Reserves football in his stride.

Name: Jack Barmby

Birthdate: 14 November 1994

Birthplace: London
Position: Winger

Son of former England international Nick, Jack Barmby is an exciting young left winger who thrives on responsibility. While versatile enough to play as a striker – where he top-scored for the under-18s in 2011/12 – it is his speed, trickery and proactive approach to the game which marks him out as a thrilling prospect on the left flank. Jack has a knack for scoring spectacular goals and bagged in every round of the FA Youth Cup as United reached the 2012 semi-finals. Whichever position he adopts in the coming years, Barmby is most certainly a burgeoning talent worth watching.

Name: Michael Keane

Birthdate: 11 January 1993

Birthplace: Stockport
Position: Defender

The 2011/12 campaign was a breakthrough season for powerful defender Michael Keane. The England youth international, who is twin brother of Reds striker Will, benefited from a substantial growth spurt and established himself as one of the most dominant, decisive young central defenders in the country. His superb form was rewarded at the end of the season when he was named Denzil Haroun Young Player of the Year, and he is a leading contender to embark on a loan deal in the near future as he looks to further his footballing education.

Spot the Difference

Can you spot the 6 differences between the two celebration photographs?

Answers on page 60

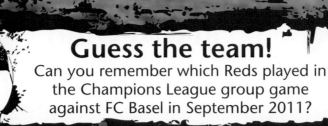

Guess the team!

Can you remember which Reds played in the Champions League group game against FC Basel in September 2011?

Three questions on...

Phil Jones

1. Against which team did Phil score his first United goal?

2. Who did Jones make his international debut against for England?

3. What is his middle name?

David De Gea

1. How many games did David play for the Reds during his debut campaign in 2011/12 35, 37 or 39?

2. How many clean sheets did he keep?

3. Which European club competition did David win with his former club Atletico Madrid?

Answers on page 60

51

Red Rewind
10 April 2007
United 7 Roma 1

**Old Trafford Champions League
quarter-final, second leg**

On a famous night at Old Trafford in April 2007, the Reds beat Roma 7-1 in the Champions League quarter-final, second leg, but what can you remember about the game?

Q1 Who opened the scoring for United?

Q2 What was the score at half-time?

Q3 Which United midfielder missed the game through suspension after his first-leg red card?

Q4 Who scored Roma's solitary goal?

Q5 What was the final score on aggregate at the end of the game?

Answers on page 60

Who's going to score?

Wayne Rooney, Nemanja Vidic and Ashley Young are all hoping to find the back of the net but only one of them can make it through the opposition's defence – can you work out who will score?

Answers on page 61

Guess Who?
Can you make out the three United stars this photo?
Answers on p60

Goal Machine
How many goals in all competitions has Rooney scored in each season at United?
Answers on page 61

2010/11 ___ Goals

2009/10 ___ Goals

2011/12 ___ Goals

2006/07 ___ Goals

2008/09 ___ Goals

2004/05 ___ Goals

2007/08 ___ Goals

2005/06 ___ Goals

WORDSEARCH

Hidden in the wordsearch below are the surnames of 10 United players. Can you find them?

DE GEA
EVRA
FERDINAND
JONES
KAGAWA
ROONEY
SCHOLES
SMALLING
VALENCIA
VIDIC

K	A	G	A	W	A	H	V	R	R
R	H	P	V	A	R	J	D	S	O
K	T	R	R	I	H	D	C	Q	O
R	V	V	A	L	D	H	M	D	N
R	E	T	E	N	O	I	K	G	E
L	N	T	G	L	X	F	C	V	Y
V	A	L	E	N	C	I	A	M	H
R	G	S	D	S	E	N	O	J	C
X	F	E	R	D	I	N	A	N	D
J	C	G	N	I	L	L	A	M	S

Words can go horizontally, vertically, diagonally, and backwards
Answers on page 61

Spot the Ball

Can you work out which ball – headed goalwards by Scholes - ends up in the net?

Red Teasers

1 What landmark did Ryan Giggs celebrate in the game at Norwich in February 2012?

2 How many goals did Paul Scholes score in 2011/12 after coming out of retirement?

3 What nationality is Jonny Evans?

4 In what year did Michael Carrick join the Reds?

5 Who is older – Phil Jones or Chris Smalling?

6 Against which team did Smalling make his United debut?

7 Antonio Valencia won the club's Goal of the Season award in 2011/12 for his strike in the 2-0 win at Blackburn in April 2012 – who scored United's other goal in that game?

8 How many FA Cups has Sir Alex won?

9 In what year did he win his first?

10 Who scored the Reds' final goal of the 2011/12 season?

Answers on page 61

Quiz answers

Spot the difference page 52

Guess the team! page 53

Back row (L-R) De Gea, Jones, Ferdinand, Valencia, Welbeck, Anderson

Front row (L-R) Carrick, Evra, Fabio, Giggs, Young

Three questions on... page 53

Phil Jones – 1. Aston Villa; 2. Montenegro in October 2011; 3. Anthony

David De Gea – 1. 39 games; 2. 15 3. The Europa League

Red Rewind page 54/55

1. Michael Carrick 2. United 4 Roma 0 3. Paul Scholes 4. Daniele De Rossi 5. United 8 Roma 3

Who's going to score? page 56

Ashley Young

Guess who? page 57

David De Gea's hair

Patric Evra's eyes

Michael Carrick's mouth and chin

Goal machine page 57

2004/05	17
2005/06	19
2006/07	23
2007/08	18
2008/09	20
2009/10	34
2010/11	16
2011/12	34

Wordsearch page 58

```
K A G A W A  H V R  R
R H P V A R J D S  O
K T R R I H D C Q  O
R V V A L D H M D  N
R E T E N O I K G  E
L N T G L X F C V  Y
V A L E N C I A  M H
R G S D S E N O J  C
X F E R D I N A N D
J C G N I L L A M S
```

Spot the Ball page 59

Red Teasers page 59

Q1 It was Ryan's 900th game for United

Q2 Four goals

Q3 Northern Irish

Q4 2006

Q5 Chris Smalling

Q6 Chelsea in the CommunityShield

Q7 Ashley Young

Q8 Five

Q9 1990

Q10 Wayne Rooney

Where's Fred the Red?

Can you spot Fred in this photo?

E IMPOSSIBLE DREAM SIR ALEX